The Varnished Truth

The Varnished Truth

Woodie Sallis

VANTAGE PRESS
New York

This is a work of fiction. Names, characters, places, and incidents either are the product of the author's imagination or are used fictitiously. Any resemblance to events or persons, living or dead, is entirely coincidental.

For Chipa

The Varnished Truth

1

Spring is like a strong-legged young man—bursting out in all directions with quick energy—striding across winter's land, young face aglow with eagerness and with earnestness.

One day in 1932, spring came to a town called Melville. Came on warm winds washed in by rivers of sunshine to spread itself over the town and over its people.

The winds were soft, the sun warm, and the people of Melville took notice of the coming of spring.

So had gone the days and years in Melville. There had been few major changes, for that matter, there were few minor ones. The human race moved relentlessly forward toward—what? Tonight, tomorrow, and next year. Always what they sought seemed just out of reach. Time healed and hurt again and healed again. March turned into April into October. A boy grew and stretched his muscles, wanting to try them all. A man grew older watching fearfully his muscles relax, hoping that one would remain still strong. Bourbon whiskey warmed the blood and a woman's oil brought relief until morning. Children were born wrinkled, red, and squalling—born out of a night's pleasure, and nurtured by duty and/or love. A few old ones died and were publicly mourned for a day or two. Buried soon and forgotten, brushed into oblivion by time's relentless pressure. Women conceived and clutched their bellies. Men fornicated and slapped their thighs—time and time and time again. Each strong back-arching thrust reaching, reaching for the future, for immortality—for tomorrow.

Herbert Hoover was President of the United States in 1932. Many of the men in Melville and in the surrounding countryside went rabbit hunting several times each week to have meat on the table for their families. They had named the rabbits Hoover Hogs. Some of the coarser men said of a local woman that she would go to bed with you just to have some meat in her stomach. There were 12 million unemployed in the U.S. National income in 1932 was exactly half what it had been in 1929. In 1932, minimum wage had not been mentioned. It was not until July 12, 1933, that minimum wage legislation was passed, requiring a pay rate of 40¢ per hour, $16 for a 40-hour week. And for most of the children of the Melville families, the bitter knife of poverty had plunged into their hearts, leaving scars. The effect of these years upon the children was to develop in them an insane niggardliness, an insatiable love of money—at least a love of acquiring it—cash money.

On this particular spring day in 1932, on Main Street of Melville, which was two blocks long and ran parallel with the railroad tracks, three men sat on a long bench in front of Stein's Department Store—the store that was the hub of the wheel of Melville, a small Southern town. The residents spoke of Stein's as the hub, even though it occupied only a corner of the actual center. Across the street east of Stein's, was the other main trading center of the town, Wener's.

Exactly opposite Stein's was the depot of the Missouri Pacific Railroad. On the other corner, east of the depot, was a vacant spot made into a flower bed by the good ladies of the local Garden Club.

Billy Bracken, attorney-at-law, by virtue of a mail-order diploma, sat there with Dave Pollard, who lived a mile out of town in a colonial mansion his father had built. Between them sat Abe Stein, the owner of the store. The fact that Abe was sitting was unusual, for he was known as "a man on the move." But spring was in the lungs and all being in their thirties, it stirred them and they felt it and were quiet for a while, just letting the sun warm them.

A few farm trucks drove noisily down the street. A few wagons lumbered slowly by, driven by Negroes known by all three. Very few people were out and all three looked up when they heard the sharp tapping of a woman's high heels on the sidewalk. Earnestine Jones, her light copper skin set aglow by the evening sun, came about and stopped.

"Mr. Bracken," she said, "you be home in a few minutes fuh suppah?"

The other two men looked quickly at Bill who smilingly replied, "Yes, Earnestine—in a few minutes."

"All right, suh. I'll have it ready."

Earnestine nodded to Abe and Dave, murmured an almost unintelligible "Yassuh" to their greeting, and walked on by them, her small hips switching naturally.

Everybody in town thought they knew or wanted to know more than they did about Bill Bracken and his cook, Earnestine. Since Earnestine occupied the servants house in back of Bill's bachelor home and since he showed no interest in any of the local belles, the town's females drew their own conclusions. But no one, not even the town booze heads, ever mentioned any of the gossip to Bill.

A 1932 model Buick drew to the curb, a blonde head poked around the side glass, and Josephine Sessions spoke; "Dave, come on home to supper." Josephine Sessions was, as everybody knew, Dave's "girl." She spent most of her time in the Pollard home outside of town with Dave and his widowed mother, Mrs. Dave Pollard, Sr. She was referred to as a "house guest," a "friend of the family," and many other polite names, but she was not married to

Dave. She lived there at the mansion in the guest room, waiting for Mrs. Dave Sr. to die so that she could become Dave Jr.'s wife.

Dave arose, giving a jaunty wave of his hand to the others, and stepped into the Buick. Bill Bracken got up, stretched, yawned, gave Abe Stein an affectionate pat on the back, and walked slowly east toward his home and supper and Earnestine. Abe stood a moment smiling to himself, his black eyes dancing as he watched his two friends turn homeward. Then he turned and entered his store, walking briskly back to the cash register.

Abe was not tall, but he walked tall. His one clerk, Miss Annie Mae Maxton, was bent over the counter near the cash register, her buttocks turned upward. With a soft laugh, Abe slapped and Miss Maxton gave a shriek and jerked upright.

"Mr. Abe! I do declare! Suppose somebody saw you!"

"Now, Annie, nobody's here. Let's lock up and I'll drive ya home. Okay?"

"Mr. Abe, everytime you do, people seem to stare at me—afterwards."

"Now, Annie, nobody's staring."

"But Mrs. Stein said the other day that I ought to walk more—."

"To hell with Mrs. Stein. My wife's got nothing to do with this. Let's get ready."

All the time that he was talking, Abe was quickly moving about the floor, spreading yards of cotton sacking material over mounds of pants stacked on counters. With quick nervous movements, he was, as he often remarked, "converting a marketplace into a mausoleum." When the last white cover was in place, the store had a somewhat sterile look. Abe's thoughts, as he watched Annie's movements, were not sterile.

This then was the beginning of an evening in spring 1932 for three men in Melville, population 1,087.

2

The people who met Billy Bracken as he strolled homeward probably thought his mind was roaming over some legal technicality as he smiled and nodded to all. His mind was doing no such thing. His thoughts were going forward as they had done for two years now to a drink, a pleasant meal in the quiet solitude of his large but unpretentious home—and Earnestine.

Earnestine was nineteen; a country Negress who knew how to please a man. Her smile was soft, her laugh was quick, and yet always there was dignity in her manner and in her movements.

When Billy entered through a living room furnished with Victorian furniture, he found the dining-room table set and his bourbon and water beside his plate.

"Earnestine," he said as he sat down and picked up the drink, "what's for supper?"

"Mr. Billy, you know you alls gets steak on Friday," replied Earnestine in a mock scolding tone.

"You say we do?"

"Stop teasing me now, Mr. Billy."

There was a small table set up in the kitchen near the door that separated the dining room from the kitchen. Under this arrangement Billy could talk over the day's happenings with his cook while observing all the local customs of complete segregation.

Pushing back his plate, Billy rose, stretched, and

walked slowly into the kitchen. His hand moved lightly across Earnestine's shoulders as he walked by. At his touch she stopped all movement, waiting.

"In about five minutes, Earnestine." That was all he said and it required no answer.

Billy walked back across the living room into the large bedroom and carefully pulled the shades all the way down to the window sills. He did not turn on any lights. He simply slowly removed all his clothing, thinking of the pleasure to come. He lay down on his naked back, throwing his muscular arms up and back, waiting.

Dusk had settled over the town. When she glided through the half-open door, Earnestine was like a moving shadow. The shadow became larger as she pulled her dress off and neatly piled her clothes at the foot of the bed. *She must have eyes like a cat,* he thought. *Yeah, and I'm old Tom himself.*

His turn of thought brought a low chuckle from his throat and he heard the soft movement of her bare feet on the carpet. No words were spoken. She leaned over him, slowly lowering her body onto his, making small sounds in her throat, her body twisting and turning against him expertly as he had taught her. She arched her buttocks upward and guided by his expert fingers, she sank slowly down again, pressing at last quickly down until he moaned with the physical pain of it. And now he did not think at all. He brought his arms quickly around to grasp her buttocks with tensed hard fingers. *Old Tom Cat! Jesus!* He closed his eyes tight and laughed deep in his throat.

Night followed dusk. The stars came; the stars twinkled.

Mrs. Stein, walking home with Abe from the movie, mildly wondered why Billy Bracken's cook was still washing dishes at 9:30 in the night.

3

One mile outside town, the Pollard mansion sat looking down over a wide expanse of green lawn, staring between the spaces of four giant colonial pillars of gleaming white. Old Judge Pollard had built it in 1920 when he was County Judge. Built it with graft money filtered into his pockets by the contractors who had built twenty-five miles of concrete highway from the Mississippi River to the Law County line. The highway split his thousand-acre cotton farm right down the middle, but with his new house, the old judge still sat on the high bench, looking down.

Josephine Sessions drove her Buick under the carport (added in 1930), and she and Dave entered through the side door. Old Mrs. Pollard, then sixty, and possessed of an icy reserve, sat by the east window. She sometimes resented Josephine's presence. But at other times she felt a need for her. She thought often of the time Dave first brought her there. That was twelve years ago when Josephine was a girl of fourteen. Sometimes she told herself the end justified the means. After she had put the town busybodies in their places with a few steely remarks. Yes, it was better this way. Two chocolate-colored images of young Dave out in the cook's house was all the proof she needed that Dave had to have female companions. But who would have thought that a boy of fifteen would—.

She cut short her musings as Dave and Josephine entered.

"Dave," Mrs. Pollard said. "I told Theolo to set supper in the breakfast room."

"All right, Mother," Dave replied, seating himself and opening his newspaper.

Josephine went slowly up the circular stairway to her "guest" room. After redoing her face, she came down in time to walk behind Dave and his mother as they entered the large pine-paneled breakfast room, just off the kitchen. Their supper was served by Theolo, a well-formed Negress who only spoke when directly addressed. In the Pollard household, meals were substantial. This one included fried chicken, heavy "sawmill" gravy, creamed potatoes, english peas, biscuits, iced tea, and for dessert, cherry cobbler. Mrs. Pollard enjoyed watching her only son eat, just as she had enjoyed watching her husband eat after they had clawed their way up to land of their own, money of their own, a "position" in life when the judge was elected.

Dave's sister, Mary, ten years his junior, was away in Memphis for a rest at the clinic. Mrs. Pollard seldom thought much about Mary. Even that terrible accident down at Squaw Bay last year when Mary's husband drowned—even that could not arouse in Mrs. Pollard the maternal feeling for Mary that she had for Dave. A son gave a woman a purpose in life. Mrs. Pollard did not care much for women. Not even her own daughter, Mary.

"Dave," Mrs. Pollard began as she folded her napkin and carefully placed it beside her plate, "these two boys of Theolo's didn't go to the field after school today. When I asked her about it, she said you told her they didn't have to work until school is out." It was more a question than a statement.

"That's all right, Mother, I did."

"Now, Dave, you know your father's theory about a nigger who won't work. He allus said if they won't work, they can't eat."

"Mother, let's get this straight. I'm running the farms. I'll tell the boys what to do."

Josephine had long ago lost all feeling of embarrassment when Dave's half-black offspring were discussed. She sat now half-smiling, waiting for the discussion to end in an argument. Mrs. Pollard lifted her head slightly and fixed strong blue eyes on her son.

"Dave, I know you manage the farms. I run them. I own them. I will have something to say about which hands I feed and work, and which I *don't!*" She emphasized every word carefully and distinctly.

"Mama," (Dave paused deliberately, knowing the use of this word could always bring his *Mother* around.) "I know you own the land and the house and me. I know Poppa left his will fixed so I can't marry 'til you—'til you've passed on. But—Theolo's—uh—boys will not be put in the field until school is out! Is that clear? Or would you want me to spell it out?"

Quickly Mrs. Pollard raised her hand and smiled. She did not like the turn the conversation was taking. Knowing Theolo's twins were her grandsons was one thing. Having them called that to her face by her son at her own supper table was something else.

"All right, Dave! All right! Let's change the subject." *Retreat, retreat from this hateful subject,* she thought.

Turning her attention to Josephine, she changed her tone of voice, even her facial expression as she sailed full tilt into "woman's talk."

"Josephine, dear, Mary phoned this evening to say she'll be home tomorrow. I wish you'd see to having her room aired tomorrow and cleaned. Will you get in behind Theolo in the morning and see to it?"

"Yes. Yes, I will, Mrs. Pollard," Josephine replied. Her voice was soft and had more of a lazy slurred country sound than Mrs. Pollard's voice. Mrs. Pollard had mastered the trick of suiting her voice to the one with whom she was talking. Josephine had not quite reached the "quality" in her speech that Mrs. Pollard would have preferred.

The talk drifted from one thing to another until nine o'clock when Dave mumbled goodnight and walked upstairs to his bedroom. Mrs. Pollard slept downstairs in the back bedroom, but lately she had been staying up long after the others in her house had gone to bed. She could think and plan better when all was quiet and dark.

"Good night, Mrs. Pollard."

"Good night, dear."

Mrs. Pollard could hear Josephine close the door behind her as she entered the guest room across the hall from Dave's room. Mrs. Pollard walked over, switched off the living room lights, and took her seat by the window where she could see the moonlight filtering down through two huge cedars onto her lawn. Only a few minutes passed before she heard the cautious click of a slowly opened door. Her hearing was still acute enough to hear sounds made by two bare feet on the hall rug and then another slight squeak of a door.

As she listened to the night noises close in around her, she reached at least one decision: she knew now that she would have to replace those old coil bedsprings in Dave's room. There was a time when the furious squeaking of bedsprings was like music, but she told herself, not any more. That son of hers, and she smiled thinking it, must be spirited in more ways than one.

4

Abe Stein was a worrier, true to his heritage. The town often said worrying made him rich. Abe could not stand to be beaten either in business or personal ventures. Abe had to win. Abe was six inches taller than his father who stood an even five feet in his stocking feet. But he stood ramrod straight, taking advantage of every inch.

Old Samuel Stein, his father, had come to Melville in 1918 with a pack of wares on his back. He had opened a small dry goods store and it had slowly prospered and grown. So had his family. Samuel, "the Daddy of them all," had four sons and three daughters, all married. One son was a doctor, one a lawyer, and one a cotton merchant in Memphis, and Abe who ran the store, managed the farms. Abe—who had his feet solidly set on top of the small holdings—determined to build an empire for the Steins.

Abe had married a Gentile, yet her name was Sarah. Her enemies said she was the biggest Jew in town (there were only three Jewish families). Outwardly, Abe was everybody's friend and his business cards read " 'Honest' Abe Stein, Merchant and Seed Buyer."

Two years ago when the Depression drained away all the fat from the small town, Abe, to supplement his income, had become the seed buying agent for Swift & Company. Using that as a wedge, he had acquired stock in three cotton gins, and this year he had hopes of muscling in on a few more. Abe was thirty-eight years old, but he still showed the proper filial respect by kissing his father every morning on arrival at the store. If Samuel stayed until closing, Abe kissed him goodnight.

Sarah was a beautiful woman. Tall, slender, but rounded and totally feminine. She had black hair and hazel eyes. It was only her pug nose that kept her from really belonging to the family into which she had married.

This spring night in 1932, Abe and Sarah were walking home from the movie, taking, as they often did, the long way home. Walking over to Silk Stocking Row, then down and back across to their home.

Sarah repeated her idle question, "Abe, I wonder why Earnestine is still washing dishes at 9:30?"

"Billy probably ate late, Sarah."

Abe was smiling to himself as they strolled home along the darkened street. There were street lights but only one at each street intersection.

"Did you like the show, Abe?"

"Yeah, it was all right. We should have taken the girls instead of leaving them with Carrie."

"Well, they need to go to bed early, and Carrie just sits there to be sure—."

"Sarah, do you realize that Miriam will graduate and be ready for college in three more years?"

"My, how time flies!"

They entered their red brick house and sent Carrie on back to her servant's house on the back of the lot.

Abe didn't always discuss minute details of business with Sarah, but thinking of his two daughters, Miriam and Sarah Jr., who was thirteen, he felt the need to assure his wife that he was thinking and planning ahead.

"Sadie," (his pet name for her) Abe began, "the store has weathered the storm so far. We'll make a little money this year. This fall I want you to cashier and help out in the busy season. That'll save hiring a girl and I don't trust just anybody with the money. That 1000-acre tract we foreclosed in '30 is looking up. I'm letting old 'Fatty' Maxton manage the sharecroppers this year. He won't cost me much and he knows how to raise cotton. However, I've got an idea about how I can pay part of our girls' college. You know Noel Arm who married the Anderton girl, Mede? Well, he's used up her inheritance raising those two boys up this far and last year he started an insurance agency. His two biggest customers are me and Joe Wener. Without us he can't stay in business. I think he'll grow with the town with our help. Sunday I'm going down to his little place with Joe and lay our cards on the table. And I want one-fourth of that young concern in return for throwing more business his way. Joe and I get one-fourth each or he's out of business."

"But, Abe, what will folks say? Won't they say you robbed him?"

"Folks—Hell! They'll say Abe is a crook, a rascal, and a son of a bitch! But you wait. They'll be glad to borrow his money, I betcha!"

Sarah merely smiled and started preparing for bed. She had long ago decided which course to pursue with the town versus Abe's deals. She smiled mysteriously at the town just as she smiled at Abe. No one knew what her thoughts were. In fact, in her occasional daydreams, Sarah saw herself as quite a Mona Lisa—enigmatic. Melville with its long-tongued living and eternal watchfulness, lived and watched—and waited.

5

Noel Arm Sr. was tall, thin, and slightly bald. He smoked incessantly and drank frequently. His wife Mede, was a plump, motherly looking woman of unusual intelligence and education. Her father had been principal of the Melville high school for twenty years and the family, though eccentric, was respected, because of its obvious superiority in intelligence and fiber.

Noel and Mede lived on the opposite end of Main Street from Abe Stein—lived in a yellow three-bedroom clapboard with their two boys, Noel Jr. and A.P., aged fifteen and thirteen.

Noel Jr. was the image of his father, except that Junior stuttered so badly he could hardly be understood. As he tried desperately to talk, his eyes batted rapidly, his mouth hung ajar and quivered as his tongue fought for control. There was within him a lost and stricken thing he could not find. Some remembered that Mrs. Arm had breast-fed him until he was almost two. The people who had no college education said Mrs. Arm's belief in the advanced ideas of modern education, meaning no discipline, was to blame. The men who hung around the drugstore, owned by Mede's brother, found his manner disturbing and somehow embarrassing. The Junior High school group was accustomed to him. He was Noel Jr. and he stuttered. They were cruel and kind to him in turn as all children are cruel and kind. The boys his own age did not always know how to re-

15

act, so they mostly kept him at a distance. The girls his own age found his affliction fascinating and frustrating at the same time. They romanticized about him, they whispered about him to each other. They liked having him along if just a group of girls was together.

Miriam Stein was possibly the prettiest girl in town. She had a Japanese tilt to her eyes and a blue-black hair line. Her features were her father's, but "on her they looked better" was often said with a wink and a smile.

6

The American Legion Hut was overflowing with light, looking like a huge lantern plopped down in the middle of town. It was Friday night and the Mothers' Club was sponsoring a dance for the teenage children.

Entering the hut, Noel Jr. held onto Miriam's arm with a tenseness he always felt in a crowd. He tried to appear calm and natural, as if he belonged at a dance like this, where all the boys wore coats and ties and most of the girls had on evening dresses. Noel felt that everybody was looking at him. He knew that he was blushing.

A short thick-haired masculine arm reached for their tickets. It was Buddy McAimes, one year older than Noel and captain of the high school football team. Buddy grinned at them, winked slyly at Noel, and Noel blushed even more as Buddy gave Miriam's neat figure a quick appraisal.

They turned to the left where all the chaperons were sitting, smiling and chatting.

"Let's go over and speak to everybody!" Miriam exclaimed. "Yeah!"

Noel could tell Miriam knew he felt out of place, self-conscious, and totally unsure of himself. Maybe she was just silently laughing at him, and later she would talk about him to other girls. *If she did—let her*—he thought, in a defiant mood. He wished the dance was over or that he hadn't come in the first place. He determined that if trying could

17

do it, he would get through. Maybe if he just danced and didn't have to talk very much—.

The juke box started, a slow rhythm. *Good,* thought Noel. Now he got warmed up, to feel the music, to forget everything except the music. His confidence increased as he glided smoothly across the floor. Hell, he *was* a good dancer. Look at Buddy trying to dance with Laura, a thin, tall, pale blonde. Why, he was plodding along listlessly. Buddy might be a big deal on the football field, but this dancing was where Noel could show him a thing or two.

The Hut was rectangular-shaped and the walls were bare of decorations. Noel danced more easily. He held Miriam closer to him. The mere touching of her in the dance postures excited him. His glance kept wandering to Buddy and Laura. Buddy was doing better now. His thick broad shoulders were squared. He had Laura crushed up against him. Noel could see Buddy's leg pushing up against her, between her legs, on the long dance steps. He wondered if Buddy also had a half hard on. Immediately he was ashamed of his thoughts. His mother had told him he must not think about such things.

The dance was over. Noel folded his arms, self-conscious. He unfolded them. He took Miriam over to the chaperon's side, excusing himself. He walked back to the men's room and entered. Buddy was there, taking a leak in the one commode. Noel stuttered a greeting.

Buddy said, "Step right up, there's room for two." Noel looked at Buddy's exposed maleness. He took out his. He stammered and strained. No stream came. He muttered he guessed he didn't need to after all.

Buddy pulled out a pint of wine hidden behind the commode and took a long swig. He passed the bottle to Noel. Noel drank and, fighting the urge to cough, he drank much more than he had planned. He didn't like wine, but the one word he despised would be hurled at him, he knew, if he refused. The single bare light bulb shone brightly above them. Buddy said he had hot pants and sure wished he knew where he could get some. Noel laughed self-consciously, and he noticed the way hair curled up on the back of Buddy's fingers.

Sometimes Noel's thoughts frightened him. He thought about girls and was ashamed of what he thought. He couldn't imagine doing anything like *that* to Miriam. But here in the toilet with Buddy, he really enjoyed the vulgar humor, the dirty talk, the visions that this talk generated. He felt more a part of the world of men.

Buddy pulled out a pack of Camels. Noel declined. Buddy puffed, curling his mouth down as he took a drag. Noel put his arm around Buddy's shoulder in a quick show of camaraderie. Buddy, wise Buddy, looked up quickly and winked. Noel was puzzled, but he liked the feeling of fellowship the talk and the wine gave him.

Two more boys came in, laughing and talking. The mood was shattered.

The music started. Buddy took Miriam. Noel hesitated, then headed for Laura. He swept across the floor in full command of every note. It made him feel good to be a part of the crowd of dancing boys and girls. He was somebody—he was Noel Arm Jr., dancer, charmer, man-about-town.

The dance ended. Buddy suggested that he and Laura take Noel and Miriam home.

During the three-block drive to Miriam's house, Noel moved closer to her. She pushed him back and started talking. Noel took her to her door. They took Laura home. Looking from the back seat, Noel tried to see if they hugged and kissed. It was too dark. He hoped they did not. Buddy slid back into the driver's seat, saying, "Let's drive around."

Noel mumbled, "Okay," as he changed to the front seat. They drove toward Buddy's house out by the graveyard. Buddy pulled the car up inside the graveyard gate and stopped. Switching off the car lights, he pulled out the wine. Noel took a long drink, feeling the liquid warm his stomach.

Buddy said, "Hell, leave me some." Noel laughed and passed the bottle to Buddy. Buddy drained it, saying, "Ain't it good." Noel decided to take a Camel. Buddy lighted it for him, cupping the match, looking directly into Noel's eyes. Noel felt strange.

The moonlight filtered through the cemetery trees. They talked and smoked. The wine flamed up through their veins. Noel could see Buddy's left hand resting in his crotch. Buddy turned sideways under the wheel, facing Noel, saying, "I like you." Noel felt confused and uncertain. Buddy's knee brushed against Noel's leg and he shivered. Quickly taking a long drag on his cigarette, Noel flipped it out the window. Buddy reached over and rubbed his hand back and forth through Noel's hair, tousling it. Noel was unsure about what was expected of him. But he wanted desperately to please Buddy. He waited. Buddy reached for Noel's left hand and slowly drew it up his leg. Noel tensed but did not protest. He was surprised to find that Buddy's pants were unbuttoned and his hard on was exposed. Cupping his hand around Noel's hand, Buddy eased the hand on down around his balls.

Noel whispered, "Your nuts are big."

Buddy said, "Yeah, do you like them?"

Noel whispered, "Yeah." Buddy removed his own hand, leaving Noel's soft hand gently massaging. Buddy leaned back on the car door and scooted toward Noel, slipping his pants and shorts down at the same time.

"Now," said Buddy.

"Now, whaat—" Noel began. Buddy cursed under his

breath. His powerful arms shot up, his fingers locked in Noel's hair. With gentle but sure pressure, he pulled Noel's head over onto his naked belly. Noel opened his mouth to say something, anything. Buddy's thumbs stopped the out-flow of words and guided his face—down. Noel closed his eyes tight, trying desperately to follow instructions, coming amidst moans as Buddy writhed toward him.

7

Sunday morning following the dance, Abe Stein and Joe Wener met Noel Arm, Sr. in the office in back of Abe's store. Billy Bracken was there too. Abe was Noel's biggest insurance customer. When Abe called, Noel felt he had to go, though he hated to give up his Sunday morning sleep.

Abe did the talking. He talked fast, in short bursts of sentences. It was quickly and firmly explained to Noel that his two biggest customers were about to become his partners unless he wanted them to start their own insurance agency. For the first few minutes, Noel's mind frantically searched for a way out. It was futile. He very quickly realized that. They had him. He signed the agreement Billy Bracken had drawn up.

Abe went home to brag to Sarah. Joe went home to explain to his wife what a big deal he'd pulled off. Noel went home to Mede and his two boys minus one half of his business and stripped of his pride. Noel Jr. was in the bathroom. For the past two days, it seemed to Mede, he had stayed in the bathroom. Noel Sr. tried to remember how it had been with him when he was fifteen. He wanted to be a proper father to his son, to understand him, to help when help was needed. Only he could not remember. Especially this morning he could not remember. Right now all he could remember was that he had an unfinished pint stuck behind the bathtub and he needed a drink.

"Noel, come out of there!" he yelled, his voice harsh.

Mede came rushing up. He banged on the door. Noel Jr. opened the door, looking very frightened, standing there with just his jockey shorts on. He tried to stutter an answer to his father. No words came. Only a quick opening and closing of his mouth. His eyes were red. Mede put her arm around her son's waist. He shook her off and ran to his room, slamming the door. Noel Sr. entered the bathroom. He drained the pint bottle, turned, entered his bedroom, and shut the door. He stretched out across the bed and was instantly asleep.

Mede stood there feeling lost, alone, helpless. Sometimes she thought her family lived behind closed doors. Everybody had a door he could slam except Mede. She could shut none of them out of her life. They were part of her—her husband, her boys. Especially Noel Jr., her first born, her baby. Her heart ached.

8

The Melville High School sat west of town on a two-acre plot of ground. The two acres had been deeded to the city by Buddy McAimes' grandfather many years ago when two acres was nothing to the land-rich McAimes family. The school, which housed and taught all twelve grades, was a square-fronted two-storied, brick structure set squarely in the middle of a two-acre field. To the west was the football field; and in season, the baseball field. To the south was the basketball court, and a small, very small, public library. There were four catalpa trees and a brick sidewalk in front of the building. An almost vacant side was on the north. There were two horizontal bars, and attached to the building, was an all-steel slide-type fire escape. The fire escape was used by the "upper" classes as the fastest way to make an exit. Every noon bell and every 3:30 P.M. bell was followed by a group of yelling, whooping, sliding students, mostly boys. The girls beat their hasty retreats down the back stairs that spilled them out on the south side or by the front stairs that wound down to the hallway and to the front entrance. At the back of the hallway was the auditorium.

Miss Ellen Rice always said Monday morning and pandemonium were synonymous at Melville High. She sat at the stage at the back of the auditorium, talking quietly with the principal while the entire student body assembled for the usual Monday morning exercises. Miss Rice taught English and Literature to the 9th, 10th, 11th and 12th grades.

She was old enough to have lost her fiancé on the *Titanic* but her exact age was guarded as closely as she tried to guard her health.

Miss Rice was many things to her students. She was firm, strict, warm, understanding, an old maid, a sweet thing, but always a good teacher. She tried to instill in her girl students all the virtues she had learned so long ago. They were her children, her only chance at motherhood, and she felt the weight of responsibility even more than most of their physical parents. Some of her students seems to require more of her, to need more of her than others.

Two of these were Miriam Stein and Noel Arm Jr. She gave a great deal of thought and hope to these two and their problems. A stranger not knowing them as Miss Rice knew them would have denied that they needed any assistance. Miriam was pretty. Her father was expected to become the richest man in town. She had poise, a superior mind still in the formative stage. But the father who gave her a promise of material security also gave her the reason for her insecurity.

She was half-Jewish, and she learned very early to erect her defenses. The wary craftiness, the quick smile, the friendly greeting, the very poise she wore—all were developed to forestall the taunt, the snicker, the pointed finger.

But if Miss Rice had been forced to choose among the students who truly needed her, she would unhesitatingly have chosen Noel. Miss Rice exhorted the fifteen-year-old boy to read Shakespeare, Coleridge, Wordsworth, to savor the wild and incoherent lines of Dante. He read them. He also read Edna St. Vincent Millay and thrilled to "My candle burns at both ends—it will not last the night. But ah, my friends, and oh, my foes, it gives a lovely light."

He read Oscar Wilde's *The Picture of Dorian Gray* and

fantasized himself the hero forever young—his evil thoughts, his evil deeds hidden upstairs on a picture. Alone he read it and laughed, squinting his eyes shut. Reading was a way to learn to jump far ahead of his contemporaries. Reading was an escape. When the life around him began to annoy and fetter him, he had only to choose a volume of words to return to a world of his own choosing. He felt the delight of solitude.

Buddy McAimes and his younger brother had the town's newspaper routes. The McAimes boys delivered both the morning and afternoon papers that came down from Memphis on the M. Pac. R.R. The whole town admired their industry and thrift and very few gave much thought to the fact that they had to get up at 4:00 A.M. to have all the *Commercial Appeals* on all the porches by breakfast time.

Saturday morning Buddy jerked awake to the swift peal of the round alarm clock. He peeled off his jockey underwear and padded naked into the bathroom. He viewed himself in the long mirror on the back of the bathroom door, grinned sardonically, and pranced stiffly up against the cold glass. He winked at himself in the mirror. *Yep, I'm a horse*, he mused, *quite a jock. Big Wheel Buddy, that's me, boys!*

He splashed cold water over his face and neck, exhaling gasps of air as the cold water brought a rush of blood to his face. Looking into the mirror, he decided not to shave until he had made the paper route. He turned his head from the towel, admired his lean hard body once more before pulling on his underwear shorts. A once white, much-laundered canvas bag, labeled *Commercial Appeal,* slung over his shoulder, he started off in a trot for the R.R. Station, a distance of approximately one mile. Whistling softly, he thought about the dance the night before. He could still hear the saxophones wailing from the records, see all the girls he'd held and danced with—Jesus, it made him hot just to think about it.

Buddy was a complete extrovert and seldom brooded about anything. But this morning he brooded, justifying his sudden impulse of last night. *Hell,* he thought *the kid's been mooning around me for a year now. He just had to be showed—a little.* Laughing to himself, Buddy hummed one of the current tunes—"My heart aches for you—," only he trotted faster as he changed heart to hard. Jesus, a guy had to do something. He felt powerful.

When he reached the R.R. Station, he noticed that Mr. Stein was already in his store working back in the office. *Funny,* he thought, *how hard that guy works.* He threw the newspaper against the front door and noticed that Mr. Stein jerked up his head at the gentle plop sound of the paper.

Buddy decided to change his usual route and to deliver in "nigger-town" last, after daylight. He never had liked to be down there while it was still dark. One of his colored customers was a bootlegger and also usually had a crap game going in the back room.

As he walked rapidly along the sidewalks, across yards, jumped over hedges—he was thinking of that time last summer when he had peeped into Miriam's room after noticing her shade was halfway up. Who would have thought she slept naked. The memory of her soft, curved white tits still stirred him. But, dammit, she must have known he looked because that was nearly a year ago and that shade had been down every morning since then.

It was 7:00 A.M. and the sun was up when Buddy returned home. His mother was in the kitchen, and Buddy hugged her from the back as he ran to wash up for breakfast.

"How was the dance, Buddy?"

"Fine, Mama. Had a good time."

"You were out late. I heard you come in."

"Yeah. I took some of 'em home."

"Well, they don't live that far away—."

"These pancakes sure are good."

"Go ahead. Change the subject."

"I just did."

"Don't be so smart, Buddy McAimes. You aren't too big to whip."

"Wanna try?"

Half amused, half belligerent. "Oh, eat your breakfast."

Buddy finished his breakfast, ducked back to his room so he could have a quick smoke, then tumbled across the bed. He drifted off to sleep, stretched flat on his stomach, one of his arms encircling the extra pillow. He slept the sleep of a tired animal.

Abe had finished checking over the books this Saturday morning, and he sat reading the *Appeal* that Buddy had left at his front door. Cotton futures were down, the stock market was down. Everything except Abe's spirit was down. Abe talked of depression, hard times, and bad luck, but in heart he was an optimist, a dreamer, a planner.

He read as he waited for his clerk, Annie Mae, and the colored porter, Jack, to arrive. He'd be happier, though, if some cash customers came in first.

This was March, and today was the day he would start giving a "Furnish" to the sharecroppers from the Big Place—fifteen Negro families to be supplied with thirty dollars worth of groceries each month for five months at ten percent interest. When Abe was mentally calculating how much he'd make from that, he always added in the profit realized on the groceries at credit prices. His mind played over these figures for a while, since he could do that and absorb the news from the paper at the same time.

The back door banged and Jack, the porter, entered.

"Mawning, Mr. Abe."

"Mawning, Jack," Abe mimicked.

"You all right dis mawning?"

"Yeah, I'm all right. Everything else is all wrong."

"Whut you mean, Mr. Abe?"

"Well, hell, Jack. Dresses are going up; pants are coming down, and everything's goin' in the hole!" There was loud laughter from Jack.

"Mr. Abe, you is a card."

"I'se gonna card you if you don't sweep this place out good and clean."

"Yassuh, I'm gonna."

With a great show of industry, Jack grabbed brooms and "turkey" dusters and started his daily chores.

Annie Mae arrived. She had just started dusting and re-arranging her side of the stock when the farm wagons rumbled up to the back door. Abe wanted the sharecroppers in early so that he could get them out of the way before the cash customers started coming in. The Negro men had brought families with them, and after about an hour of arguing, pleading, laughing, and protesting, there were fifteen separate piles of groceries on the concrete floor at the back of the store. Forty-eight pound sacks of flour, stands of lard, cans of baking powder, and boxes of soda, salt, and pepper. These staples were all that the thirty dollars would cover. Abe insisted that each family have a garden, chickens, a cow, and a few hogs. He wanted to be sure that each family got no more than they could pay for come Fall. It was 8:00 A.M. The other stores were opening. A few citizens were coming uptown. The rural customers too were arriving. Abe saw them and rushed out front to wave, to yell, to "do business."

<h1 style="text-align:center">9</h1>

Noel awoke at eight Saturday morning. He awoke slowly, almost reluctantly. He craned his neck, holding his ear with his hand. In sleep he was lost, submerged, safe. He awoke thinking the world full of mockery and menace, convinced that in a hundred secret places people gathered to mock and betray him.

Although he was guilty of a thousand such fantasies, he was also guilty of swinging suddenly to the other extreme and viewing himself as a genius. *Ah, but they do not know me, the great I. They see a stuttering fool, when in reality I am a quick-witted profound intellectual, the likes of which this town will not see again.*

He was alternately wild, careless, extravagant, mute, and afraid, his guilt heavy around him. He feared crowds with an unreasoning fear. Singly he could deal with humans. In bunches, he often thought, they are carrots, lumpy and yellow, with great clods of dirt clinging to them. He awoke at eight and got up to face another Saturday, thinking—*the done cannot be undone.*

On the east corner of Main and Concord Streets, opposite the Bank of Melville, perched the Capitol Theatre. There was a balcony for colored people, while downstairs was for whites. And on Saturday the children of Melville flocked in droves to the matinee. The price was ten cents up to age twelve; above twelve years of age the cost was twenty-five cents. Those who paid a quarter, paid in pride and repented as they passed by the popcorn stand empty-handed.

Miriam came to the Saturday afternoon matinee, brought by her mother in their Chevrolet sedan, accompanied by her sister, Sarah Jr. As they hopped to the sidewalk, big skirts swirling, they were met by squeals and giggles from the other teenagers lined up for tickets. In the line near the box office was Noel Jr. and his brother A.P. Walking up behind Miriam and Sarah, came Buddy McAimes and three other boys, all in high spirits, common to all on Saturday afternoon.

The show today was a Joan Crawford picture. The elaborate posturing and "profiling" going on in the line of girls could attest to that. The fact that Clark Gable was Joan's leading man would account for the fact that the boys self-consciously pitched their voices to a lower key. They attempted the quizzical grin, the swagger, and the eye appeal. Mothers, leaving their children, thought the show *outside* was better than the movie.

Pathé News came on and the talking and laughing died down. Seated in the third row from the front, Miriam found herself between the McAimes boys and the Arm kids. Buddy had his arm around the back of her seat and Noel kept fidgeting. *My, he is a nervous boy,* she thought. Kept peeking 'round in front of her at Buddy. Boys were so silly. Sometimes she—oh, well—here was her ideal, Joan Crawford. Miriam felt that she was no longer in her theatre seat. She was up there on the screen—she was Joan Crawford, and by stretching her imagination and adding a mustache, Buddy *could* be Clark Gable. The show was on.

Noel had entered the theatre feeling cold and depressed and unwanted. He kept his eyes downcast, said nothing, and his too-red mouth was turned down at the corners. He wanted to talk to Miriam. *I wouldn't know what to say to her. She wouldn't listen.* His thoughts twisted around him, like vines groping for anchorage and succeeding only in growing around each other. *It's too late anyway. The show is starting.*

Buddy felt good after his nap. He'd met three of his classmates in Anderton's Drug Store, and walking down to the Capitol, he felt strong, very superior, and possessed of much secret knowledge. They all eyed the girls, winked, grimaced, and made their way into the show. He had to shove a couple of kids aside to get the seat by Miriam, but he got it. Then looking around—there was that jerk Noel on the other side. Oh, well he might make time with Miriam, get in a feel or two, but Jesus—how involved could a guy get! But then when you are the man Buddy McAimes is—. Joan Crawford on screen cut into his thoughts.

The show was over. The lights blazed on. Fantasy vanished. Reality returned. Red velvet curtains closed over the magic screen. All the teenagers headed for Anderton's Drug Store for a cherry coke and some talk.

The round white tables in the center of the store were soon surrounded by giggling, laughing, shuffling boys and girls, most of them fifteen to seventeen years old. Cherry cokes were flowing from the fountain along with a few sodas and malts.

"Boy, am I out of shape," said Buddy, flexing his muscles as he swung his leg over a stool in front of the fountain.

"Too many cigarettes," commented one of his friends, making an up and down motion with his hand. The girls in back, overhearing, giggled, pretending not to understand.

Miriam and Sarah Jr. sat near the back, talking earnestly and rapidly to two other girls. Buddy ignored them elaborately. The crowd drifted out, leaving Buddy with his three friends and Noel and A.P. Buddy suggested going down to Squaw Bay for a swim. Some said it was still too cold. Buddy laughed at them and they agreed to go. Swinging around on his stool, Buddy lowered his head so that he seemed to be looking up at Noel Jr.

"Ya'll want to come?" Noel looked quickly at A.P. who said he'd better go on home. The five boys piled into Buddy's car and started the two-mile drive to Squaw Bay.

The ancient Ford whizzed along the narrow pavement, going west from town toward the boys' favorite swimming place. Of course they knew that it was too early in the spring to be going swimming. They knew the water would be chilly, probably still cold, but they were young, adventurous, high-spirited, and anxious to rid themselves for the first time this year of Winter's cumbersome clothing.

"Boy, was I ever blind Friday night," said Buddy, starting the conversation.

Noel, in the back seat, jerked his head up quickly, marshalling his defenses.

"Yeah, I saw you and Noel guzzling that wine in the toilet. Why don't you get a funnel?" answered one of Buddy's companions, whose name was Frank—a pimply-faced, slack-mouthed boy of sixteen whose blond hair was dry as straw and uncombed.

Ah, thought Noel—*ah, yes, it rains on the just and the unjust alike.* Aloud he stammered, "Yeaaah—we were pretty gone all right." Buddy turned his head toward the back seat and winked at Noel. Noel trembled and grinned slowly at the shared subterfuge.

"How'd you guys make out at the dance?" this from Frank. "Did you get plenty?" Loud laughter all around.

"Yeah, we got plenty—dancing and then plenty sleep afterwards," Buddy.

"Yeaaah." Slowly from Noel. Buddy pulled out his Camels, passed them around, and all lighted one. They were nearing the Bay now.

"Say, Buddy," asked Frank, "ain't this where ole Dave Pollard drowned his brother-in-law?"

"Well, I heard Dad and Mama talking. Dad says Dave just didn't like Mary's husband and that Dave got him drunk and pushed him into Squaw Bay so's he couldn't spend anymore of the Pollard money. Mama said the two of them drank all the time anyway and that it was probably an accident. Anyway, Dad said the insurance company paid on accidental death and that Mary now has more money than old Mama Pollard."

Another of Buddy's companions spoke up—Howard, a black-headed, clean-cut boy, who was easy going and agreeable. "Aw, you know how people talk in this town. It probably was an accident."

"My mother thinks Dave drowned him," offered Noel.

The talk stopped as the car turned off the pavement onto a dirt road and soon onto a small decline leading down to Squaw Bay. The boys were out of the car, pulling at their clothes before they noticed another car parked farther down the Bay's rim, about a half mile away. Lying in front of the car were two figures, a man and a woman.

"Say," exclaimed Buddy, "ain't that Mr. Bracken's car? And ain't that his cook there with him?" All eyes turned toward the car and the couple, but now the couple had jumped into the car and the car backed up the bank and turned toward the highway so fast they couldn't be sure.

Frank gave a low whistle, slapped his buttocks in mock glee. "That Earnestine must be some good tail. But by golly that bank'd be amighty hard place to get it." Howls of laughter.

"It's got to be hard to get it," offered Buddy slyly. "Aw, come on. Let's swim."

Quickly forgetting the interlopers, the boys stripped and walked toward the stream. Two stopped to test the water with their feet. It was cold but none among them would say that it was. They plunged in, shouting and splashing and spewing water at each other. The two who were still young enough to be embarrassed by their nakedness hurried to submerge and cover themselves with water. Buddy waded out of the water first and called for the others to follow. With deft movements of their hands, they all stripped the droplets of water from their bodies and pulled their clothing on, shivering as they buttoned up. An automobile whizzed by on the pavement in the distance. It was almost dark. An owl hooted far back in the woods. They all were suddenly very quiet, lounging around the car. A train whistled far away—a lonesome haunting sound. They were young male animals on the prowl, caught in a moment of stillness by the still bay. Life rushed on, over, and by them, but they were unaware.

10

Mary Pollard Smith came home from Memphis with a trunk full of new clothes and a head full of plans. She wanted a husband, a child, and a home of her own. Lying in the clinic, she had devised a scheme calculated to get all three for herself. Her husband, Sidnay Smith, had been her lover before they were married. His death had left her inconsolable, close to a nervous breakdown, or so the doctor said. Mary understood the meaning of the unrest that had welled up in her these past few months. Some things you could talk about to your doctor; some things you could only think about. In her thinking she arrived at her decision: Billy Bracken.

Mary was tall, blonde, and her skin was fair. She was ten years younger than Dave and smarter in many ways. Her voice had a nasal twang, but she was called "pretty" by her neighbors, who often philosophized that "anybody with that much money is pretty." She wasted no time after her arrival in implementing her plan of action. On Saturday Mrs. Dave Pollard, Sr., at Mary's insistence, called Billy Bracken and invited him over for Sunday night "suppah."

Billy was too surprised to do anything but say he'd come. The only time he had ever entered the Pollard home before was to conclude legal matters for the family. He had never been there as a regular guest. He was flattered and curious. Saturday afternoon just before dark, he had decided to drive Earnestine out to her mother's farm to stay the night. On the way out, he had the radio playing, and the music was slow and nostalgic. Earnestine began moving her legs and feet unconsciously lost in the sensual sound. She teased him with slow movements as she bit her lower lip, swaying with the music. At the Squaw Bay turnoff, he could no longer think of caution. He turned off and parked.

Billy had spent Sunday quietly, and was on his way out to the Pollard's, speculating about the invitation. He drove slowly as he passed back through town, down the main street.

Billy was not a man who spent useless time in profound thought. He often amused himself thinking about his neighbors, their dalliances, the many twists and turns they took in their pretenses. Billy was a realist—a man able to face facts about life, his life as well as the lives of people around him. He found them all, including himself, highly amusing.

All of us, he thought, *living our little white lies. Those boys*, he mused, that he had left down at Squaw Bay Saturday. *Just old enough to know a little of life but not old enough yet to partake of it. Not mellowed. Not disciplined yet.* Not old enough to plan a way of life that would be as satisfactory as the life Billy had planned for himself. He had, as the only local attorney, a position in town, a nice home, his woman, and a little money in the bank. Now, perhaps he might expand a bit, move up socially, become familiar with the Pollards. Hell, who could know? He had time and he had many talents.

Billy rang the bell and was admitted by Theolo. Now there was a delicious chocolate drop. If Earnestine ever got out of line, he might give some thought—.

"Evenin', Mr. Billy," greeted Theolo; "dey's in de livin' room." Theolo and Earnestine were close friends and of course Theolo must know many things about the Bracken household. Her manner had never betrayed that knowledge.

Dave rose to greet Billy with a handclasp. Mary rushed over, offering her hand. Mrs. Pollard remained seated, merely nodding and smiling her greeting. She had begun to sense the fact that Mary had something definite in mind concerning Billy Bracken, and she had already decided not to interfere. After all Mary was twenty-two years old and in a man's language, with which Mrs. Pollard was very familiar, Mary was second-hand merchandise on the marriage market. Dave and Billy had a bourbon and water before dinner. Conversation came easily and flowed gently around the supper table. It was quiet talk of no great significance. It filled the silent spaces with friendly sounds, masking the secret thoughts of all. That, for Billy Bracken, would have been a good definition of dinner table conversation. It filled in the spaces.

After dinner they regrouped in the living room, and Mary sat beside Billy on the French loveseat. They chatted amicably and politely. Mary suggested that Billy accompany the family to church on Sunday. Billy agreed. The pattern did not escape him. He even welcomed the chase in reverse. After all, he believed in life, liberty, and the pursuit. Let the pursuer beware! He invited Mary and Mrs. Pollard to have dinner with him the next Saturday night. They accepted eagerly and profusely. The plan was in motion and it was going much more smoothly than Mary had anticipated.

Billy told them all goodnight and began the short drive back to town. He entered his dark empty house, and after leisurely drinking another bourbon, went to bed and immediately to sleep. He slept secure in the knowledge that Earnestine would be back on Monday in time to have his breakfast ready when he awoke. He liked his orderly life, but the opportunity Mary offered was tempting.

Monday morning Earnestine had returned from the country, bringing fresh eggs for Mr. Billy's breakfast. When he emerged from the bedroom, shaved and dressed for work, she had his breakfast waiting. "Mawning', Mr. Billy."

"Morning, Earnestine. Did you enjoy your visit?"

"Yas, suh, ah did. 'Cept ah worried 'bout you not havin' nobody here to care fo' you."

"I made out all right. But this breakfast sure is good."

"Yas suh, yas suh," said Earnestine grinning, "and I'se planning you a good suppah too."

"Just don't forget what I like for dessert."

"Mistah Billy," Earnestine said in mock severity, "Ah don't know whut I'se gonna do wit you."

"I know. Want me to tell you?"

"Mistah Billy, ah declare."

"Okay Earnestine. I won't tease you anymore."

Earnestine busied herself about the kitchen, pouring Mr. Billy another cup of coffee, hovering solicitously near the table. She often remarked to Theolo that a woman ought to gain pride in taking care of her man.

As soon as Mr. Billy left for his office, Earnestine set about straightening up the house and cleaning up the kitchen. Theolo was coming over this morning to see her and she wasn't going to have Theolo see her kitchen in a mess. Theolo came bustling in the back door nearly bursting with all the news she had for Earnestine. The two colored women, finding nothing unique in their way of life, grinned and laughed and hugged each other with genuine delight. They purred at each other, each carefully choosing the moment to drop her juiciest piece of news.

They sat over coffee and cigarettes at Earnestine's table in the corner of the kitchen. Earnestine could wait no longer. "Theolo, guess whut?"

"How I goin' guess when you ain't even hinted?"

"I'se pregnant."

"Say you is!" exclaimed Theolo. "Who knocked you up?"

"You know ain't nobody but Mr. Billy."

"Lawdy! Lawdy! Lawdy! Is you tole 'im?"

"No, I ain't—yet."

"Well, you bettah and quick too."

"Why quick?" Instantly alerted by Theolo's tone, Earnestine was feeling panic.

"'Cause Miss Mary got plans fo' Mr. Billy and herself—that's why!"

Theolo had parried Earnestine's news in a more dramatic way than she ever could have planned. She was positively gloating now.

"Whut you means?"

"He was out fo' suppa Sunday night and Miss Mary near 'bout to eat 'im up. She simpering like a sixteen-year ole, she is."

"Humph!" Utter disdain in one word. "Dat washed-out white woman can't give Mr. Billy what he wants."

"Don't you reckon?"

"Naw, I don't reckon." Conviction had left her voice. Despair was in every syllable. Her Mr. Billy—her man. It had never occurred to her he might marry. What *would* she do if he did?

Earnestine had had enough news for one day. She diverted the conversation to other safer channels. They spoke of other matters and soon were joking and laughing, their very nature transporting them back into a normal world of light tone, light gossip, and loud laughter. When Theolo left, no further mention was made of Earnestine's pregnancy. As Theolo walked east toward her home, a light wind of March stirred about her. A smell of burning leaves wafted around her; people hurried about disposing of winter's leftovers.

Down the street a straggling line of boys and girls walked in Spring, walked toward home and the noonday meal. They left the concrete sidewalks to walk on springy ground, heavy and warm and spermy—holding April's promise.

As she reached the edge of town, on the left a field hand urged his mule forward and his large bare feet followed unevenly in the damp black and fallow furrow. On her right, one of Mr. Dave's tractors was also furrowing the field, but it was mechanical, removed from nature, sterile, smooth, and efficient. Theolo did not like tractors.

11

This was Monday morning and since last Friday night, Noel had read nothing. He had sat brooding in his room, feeling alternately elated and depressed. Tears had come and laughter. He had relived the events of last Friday night a hundred times. His mind had raced back and forth—rejecting—rejoicing—hating—fearing.

"What if somebody knew?" said Noel into the darkness. He could see the entire student body taunting him with careless words.

For a moment his face was full of pain and bitterness. Then, as he had done a dozen times already, when he had seared his heart with self-loathing, he remembered, as a completely detached person the events following the dance. It rose up to blot all other far-flung thoughts, and he viewed quite calmly this other Noel who was not he, whose face was white, bewildered. He saw this other Noel's face turn scarlet as he closed his eyes trying desperately to follow instructions coming amidst soft curses as Buddy slid toward him—the two Noels merged and his cry of anguish could be heard beyond the walls of his room.

Mede burst into his room, wide-eyed. Quickly, he regained his composure and told her he was having a nightmare, and that he had to get ready for school. He would be late.

Miriam ran up the school sidewalk, smiling, nodding in her quick way to all in sight. Noel walked slowly across the

42

front lawn of the school, head down, eyes darting to each side, his stomach churning. He walked up the steps and entered the hallway. Miriam greeted him, "Hi, Noel."

"Hi-i," he stuttered. He grinned self-consciously, he gulped, fighting for self-control.

She grabbed his arm and walked quickly back toward the auditorium, heading for the tenth grade section. Noel felt grateful for her attention. His mind moved up and away from himself. He was again off in a world of fantasy—head held high, eyes alert.

They sat down near the back row, which was empty. Miss Rice rapped for order. Buddy McAimes came pounding down the hall, and since he was late, he didn't walk down front to the senior row. He looked around hastily and sat down on the other side of Miriam. He leaned around Miriam to mutter at Noel, "Hi, Sport." Noel blushed, gasped. His fears vanished. The world came into focus.

Miss Rice spoke, "Boys and girls, we will have the invocation by our principal, Mr. Pate." Mr. Pate, his balding head shining under the droplight on the stage, stepped forward, revealing baggy blue serge pants, a rumpled coat, and tie askew. "Our Father who art in Heaven—."

Two hundred and forty heads were bowed, but about half the students' eyes were open and sliding back and forth—"full of the devil," Mr. Pate often said.

While the assembly was standing, the music teacher, Mrs. Larry Sims, led them through a loud "America" on the upright piano. Mrs. Sims played with gusto. In the privacy of her home and at local house parties, she banged out jazz and the popular ballads of the day. It was a credit to her self-discipline that she was able to tone down her tempo during school hours.

A few routine announcements ended the assembly and the students marched out in fire drill form, class by class. First the Seniors, and Buddy, with a wave of his hand, left Miriam and Noel to join his classmates.

The 12th, 11th, and 10th grades were in one big room upstairs on the south side of the building. The room was called Study Hall, but it served also as a classroom. All the students sat with their backs to Miss Rice who presided over the room from a large desk placed on a raised dais. She held classes by seating a class facing her in student chairs arranged in a semi-circle around the large desk. The fact that one class was in session while two other grades studied was disconcerting to performers and listeners alike. There were advantages to the arrangement too. Three echelons of student society could learn from each other.

Miss Rice had her own unique way of keeping order. While she listened to the recitations of the class grouped before her, her eyes roamed across the backs of the two others grades in "study hall." She could spot a note being passed without trying. She could pinpoint a snicker in a second. Instantly her voice (strong for one so small) would sing out, "Sam (or Joe), I've given you a check!" Miss Rice's check was a demerit. It meant staying fifteen minutes after school. Three checks meant a visit to the principal's office. Most of the students feared Miss Rice's checks more than they did expulsion from school. Those first few minutes after school were precious and vital. Buddies teamed up, couples paired, mutual friends ganged together, and after fifteen minutes a disobedient student was left to walk home by himself.

The noon bell rang and students erupted from their seats like compressed springs suddenly released. They overflowed the hallways, upstairs and downstairs, each one pressing forward, straining to get outside. The warm spring wind blew softly. The sun was bright and unusually warm for March. It was a gentle warm lazy kind of day.

The students who lived in Melville walked toward their homes for the midday meal. A few were picked up in the family car by their mothers. The country students from the outlying consolidated schools brought their lunches in paper bags and they gathered now in the auditorium to eat their lunches. Later—their laughter rang around the school playgrounds. Their shrill quick-changing voices echoed from all four sides of the big square red brick building, and Miss Rice closed her eyes tight to concentrate on the sounds she loved.

Her nervous hands pulled at the scarf around her neck. Some of the sounds, some of the heedless words made her wince. She recognized the voices making the vulgar sounds—she knew the reasons they were crude. She could not help them. Life reverberated around the old building, pounded in and out the hallways and came panting, came reluctantly back to class when she rang the one o'clock bell. She was again in command of her children.

Miss Rice watched her two favorite pupils settle into their seats. Miriam alert, sedate, a completely feminine girl of great poise, her face full of dark secret beauty. Noel Jr. walked in jerkily, eyes downcast, unsure of every move, grinning vacantly. *They are my special ones*, she thought. *These two are my special trusts.*

Buddy McAimes came in with bounding strides, arrogance showing in every step. He slid into his desk. He wiped the beaded sweat from his forehead and stared sightlessly at his opened book. *That one,* mused Miss Rice, *probably needs his mouth washed out with soap. Better still, his mind.*

The school was laced with economic segregation on the exact lines that separated the adults in town—like unto like—birds of a feather. There were essentially three groups. Children of the local merchants and the banker and children of the wealthy farmers formed the top group. Next came children of the small store owners and then of small farmers who rented or share-cropped. The lines were never crossed—the groups seldom mixed.

12

April's promise bore much fruit in May. Then on the last Friday of the month, there were three events that stirred the town into a frenzy of excitement, wonder, and speculation.

The annual graduation exercises were held in the high school auditorium. The American Legion Post sponsored a dance afterwards for the graduates and for the town. And at 5:00 P.M. Friday in the Presbyterian Church, Mrs. Mary Pollard Smith married Mr. Billy Bracken. Only the immediate families were invited.

The nineteen members of the 1932 graduating class grouped themselves in a semi-circle on the stage of the auditorium. In their black caps and gowns (rental $3.50 each), they resembled graduates everywhere. For most, the carefree days were over; for others, it was a beginning of a new freedom. Mr. Pate and Miss Rice were seated to one side of the stage. Their faces wore a mask of dignity, composure, and sedateness. The ceremony creaked along to conclusion. The audience of relatives and friends talked even during the exercises—hissing the news about Mary Pollard and Billy Bracken. Finally the graduation ceremony was over and the crowd headed toward the Legion Hut.

This Friday night dance was special. Members of the senior class and members of the junior class attended, but since it was sponsored by the American Legion, the younger married couples also attended. It was a town celebration. Those who felt they were too old to dance sat in folding chairs all around the perimeter of the dance floor. The juke box was already plugged into the electrical socket, revolving lights flashing. When all the students and graduates had arrived, Abe Stein, local Commander of the American Legion, punched the first number, "Stardust"—"Sometimes I Wonder Why"—and soft oohs and ahs were heard as couples glided onto the dance floor. Then "Cocktails For Two"—more oohs and ahs. Buddy McAimes tonight had dated Miriam, and Noel Jr. dated Laura. They danced, they swirled, then dipped, lost in the sound of the music.

When the dance was over, Buddy and Miriam were in the front seat of his ancient Ford, and Noel and Laura were in the back seat. Buddy followed the same routine he had after the last dance—Miriam home first, then Laura.

Noel, after walking Laura to her door, got into the front seat with Buddy. Each lighted a Camel and neither said anything. Buddy drove again up into the graveyard and stopped. With his right hand, he tousled Noel's hair. An hour later they drove home, each wondering what excuse he could give his parents for arriving an hour later than expected.

13

Saturday night in Melville: The streets were black with faces of the country Negroes. The town was full of their loud laughter and boisterous humor. Everybody from miles around came to town on Saturday and they stayed late, visiting, shopping, drinking, and "socializing." The mandated five-day week was unheard of, but no amount of talk could persuade a Negro to work on Saturday. It was his day and night to prowl.

Sunday in Melville: everybody slept late, even those who went to church. Slept late, breakfasted big, and it was the only day to be lazy in a lazy town. In the afternoon, still wearing their Sunday school clothes, the high school crowd descended on the small local theater.

Steins of Melville: they were a very interdependent, excitable clan—swept along by currents of inordinate attraction and affection. There were four sons in the Stein family, but it fell to Abe to stay in Melville and run the businesses. Abe was strong, dependable, possessed of maniacal energy. Short in stature, he walked tall and fast. He talked the same way—fast—with short bursts of words, tumbling over each other. Each word emphasized by quick and emphatic hand movements. His friends said that if you tied his hands, he simply could not talk. He finished the eighth grade and quit to run off with a visiting baseball team. His daddy chained him to the bedpost and there he remained until he promised not to run away. He stayed chained there four days and four nights before he decided to promise.

Mary Pollard and Billy Bracken returned after a one-week honeymoon at the Peabody in Memphis. Immediately Mary started planning her own house to the west of the Pollard mansion. She had architects, contractors, and lumber merchants come to her at the mansion. Four months later she moved into her new home and five months after that, Pollard Bracken, her son, was born.

14

Beginning of 1932—after the Wall Street collapse. Herbert Hoover was still in the White House. But to the fourteen and fifteen-year-olds in Melville, poverty seemed normal. Sure—three years ago, most of their families had more money, but at age fourteen or fifteen, who looks back? Life is today and tomorrow. Except Abe Stein. He was looking forward to the time when a Democrat became president, knowing the government would then step in to stop the country from bleeding to death.

November 8, 1932: Franklin Roosevelt was elected president of the U.S. In March 1933, FDR ordered all banks in the U.S. closed for reorganization. Now Abe moved. He put his father, Samuel, on the train to Memphis, where he borrowed from Jewish friends all the cash he could get. Samuel brought the cash back to Melville by train, in an old dilapidated suitcase, tied together with rope.

Now—Abe Stein was the only person in Melville who had any cash to speak of. Abe put the money in a large stand-up safe in the store. For extra insurance he slept in the store, armed with a shotgun, stretched out in front of the safe.

Being a positive thinker, believing in Roosevelt, he loaned the money out in both large and small parcels—at ten percent interest per month. His friends praised him.

When the banks reopened, Abe collected his principal plus interest and he was on his way to becoming the richest

51

man in town. The main highway coming into Melville was Highway 25 (yes, the same one Judge Pollard was involved with building). A Gulf filling station anchored the city limits on the east—and Highway 25 ran into and became the main residential street, where most of the socially elite and prosperous families lived. The local wags named the street "Silk Stocking Row." Abe Stein lived two streets south of Silk Stocking Row on the south side of the railroad tracks that split the town of Melville like a knife halving an apple. Abe's house was the last house at the end of the block, with a large vacant lot separating him from "niggertown." He liked to say he was from the wrong side of the tracks.

We all like to reorder memory. We want to remember our joy and not to remember the ugly parts. And so I remember Melville—a small night light winking on the vast expanse of Arkansas. A population of a thousand, give or take a few—America (rural America) in miniature. On Friday night, if you are dragging Main Street, you drive two blocks and turn around. The mainstay for some is alcohol, for the others that "Old Time Religion." Melville had four churches—Christian, Baptist, Methodist, and Presbyterian. The "first families" and the well-to-do, belonged to the Presbyterian Church. The congregation was small. The three Jewish families in town drove twenty miles to the county seat of Helmsman to attend synagogue.

15

May 1935: One of Miriam's classmates was Della Braves, one of three sisters, who lived one mile west of Melville with their widowed father, John Braves. John Braves owned a farm north of Melville, which adjoined a farm owned by Sam Barruth. On Barruth's farm lived a Negro woman with a "high yellow" complexion. She had four children who could almost "pass" for white and all of them used the last name of Barruth.

John Braves rode a horse to oversee workers on his farm, and often stopped by the Negro woman's house to get a drink of water.

On a Friday in 1935, Sam Barruth rode up just as John Braves was mounting his horse in front of the Negro woman's house. Sam Barruth fired both barrels of a double-barreled shotgun into the chest of John Braves. He died instantly.

Sam Barruth's trial was held in Helmsman, and Della and her sisters went every day to sit weeping in the courtroom. They felt deserted and degraded that their father had been murdered because of his presumed involvement with a Negro woman. Sam Barruth was sentenced to ten years in prison, having claimed self-defense.

An aunt and an uncle of the three Braves girls moved into their home to care for them.

Shortly after the trial, Wener's Department Store hired a young Jewish man from Memphis, Bennie Gold, as buyer and manager for their department store. Bennie decided to get an apartment in Helmsman and drive back and forth. The local citizens thought this was a bit strange and extravagant. Nevertheless, they continued to shop there because Wener's stocked the name brands they wanted.

Bennie Gold was twenty-four years old and single. The first time he saw Della Braves, he thought, *This is the cream of the crop in Melville.* Bennie started dating Della, and they usually went to Helmsman for dinner and a movie. On the third date, he took her to see his apartment on Stonewall Street. After that visit, it became routine—dinner, movie, visit to the apartment.

Two months after the first visit, Della told Bennie she was pregnant. When Della realized marriage was not in Bennie's plans, she agreed to an abortion by a local doctor. The doctor must not have been well qualified because she continued to bleed for three days.

Bennie resigned from Wener's and returned to Memphis. Three months later Della moved to Memphis and found an office job. A month after Della moved to Memphis, Bennie married a Jewish girl from a distinguished family.

16

The depression still enveloped all of the United States, but to the Melville High School's graduating seniors, it was a year of proms, romance, and magic.

Miriam Stein was valedictorian and Noel Jr. was salutatorian. Miss Rice was still guiding both of them. Several of the former Melville High School graduates had returned from college for the graduation exercises of 1935 and for the dance. Among them, Buddy McAimes, who attended Teachers College. He had returned to Melville every summer to renew his friendships, to review his conquests at college, to continue his relationship with Noel Jr., and to date Miriam Stein.

This year Buddy had a plan. He wanted Noel Jr. to attend Teachers College, beginning in September, and to share a room with him. That arrangement would solve so many problems for him.

The Legion Hut—blinking with light, like a huge lightning bug, drawing toward its door the crowd of graduates, visitors, and families. Abe and Sarah Stein were designated chaperons—some said sponsors. Mr. and Mrs. Billy Bracken were seated in the center of all the people ringing the dance floor. It was a town celebration—the last school dance for the 1935 Seniors of Melville High School.

Buddy and Miriam—Noel and Laura, a foursome, arrived together—laughing, joking, hurrying toward the music. Better dancers now. More mature, somehow. The parents of the seniors and other married couples sat in folding chairs around the walls of the Hut. "Stardust" was still a favorite. When the first waltz came from the juke box, some of the parents took over the dance floor. Most of the student couples danced over to the edge of the floor, leaving the middle for the parents and chaperons. The next platter, a foxtrot, gave the floor back to the students.

Sitting at the back of the Legion Hut was Virginia Mass, one of the seniors, dressed in a red taffeta evening gown. Her father had brought her because she had never been on a date. Later it was learned that she had spent months planning to attend this dance and that she had ordered the red taffeta from Sears and Roebuck, using the last dollar she had saved. Virginia sat there all evening. No one ever asked her to dance. Her father came promptly at midnight and took her home. The music was loud. The dance floor was crowded. There was much laughter and rapid talk.

In the men's toilet, Buddy was standing by the commode when Noel came in. Buddy looked up quickly and winked as he flipped his cock back inside his slacks. Noel blushed and stammered. Buddy said, "We'll take the girls home and then drive around." Noel lowered his head and nodded. Buddy reached behind the commode for the hidden bottle of wine, just as he had three years ago. They each took a drink.

At midnight the dance ended and the juke box was unplugged. Buddy and Noel escorted Miriam and Laura home and drove out to the old cemetery. Later, Noel said he would talk to his parents about the possibility of going to Teachers State. Buddy glanced sideways at him and growled.

After graduation, summer arrived quickly. Only four of the nineteen high school graduates had families with enough income to enable them to plan for college. Noel obtained a scholarship and was able to plan on joining Buddy. Miriam was accepted by Washington University in St. Louis.

Several of the graduates, knowing they could not attend college, accepted jobs in the local grocery stores, clothing stores, and shoe stores. Their weekly salaries ranged from seven to fifteen dollars. But, on Saturday night, those working and those not working, gathered at a small club, five miles east of town, called the Cricket. The juke box played and they danced until midnight. The juke box, for a nickel, would blast out dreams of romance and love and other splendors.

17

"Fibber McGee and Molly" debuted on NBC radio and on the morning after their show, they were quoted all over town. Most households had acquired a small radio, most of them oval shaped at the top, and some cost as little as five dollars.

The Dionne Quintuplets were one year old. The Federal Deposit Insurance Corporation was two years old and the Federal Savings and Loan Insurance Corporation was one year old. At last, all the banks and S&L's were safe, and the small sums people had accumulated were removed from beneath the mattress.

Amelia Earhart took off on a solo flight from Honolulu to Oakland, California, and the people of Melville were amazed that a *woman* could perform such a miracle. They kept up with national and international news via radio news and broadcasts and reading every word printed in the newspapers.

When they read about Adolph Hitler, it was like reading about a man from another planet. None of the Melville people could grasp the significance of the Little Corporal's ambitions.

The summer of 1935 was a last grasp at irresponsibility, at "play time," at the pleasure of being not quite grown-up. Several times each week, the young graduates and friends (all male) would gather at Squaw Bay to swim and frolic and to lie naked on the bank, letting the evening sun dry their bodies. It was to be the last lazy summer in their lives.

Buddy McAimes was usually the leader, the instigator of the swimming party. Here was a "college" man, and all listened as he joked and embellished the truth about his life at college. They joked and lied and laughed about the girls in Melville. One in particular they nicknamed Tooby—which one said was short for two-bits. One they named Big Easy because she was big and she was an easy lay. But this was just idle boy-talk and mostly made up lies.

Noel Jr. usually accompanied the group of swimmers because Buddy insisted. One day the boy named Frank said, "Whatta ya want him along for? He's either a nut or a fruit or both." With one blow Buddy bloodied Frank's nose and knocked him to the ground. No more objections were heard.

During the summer of 1935, Buddy had started also to date a girl named Ruth, whose family had moved into Melville to open a rooming house. She was small, perky, and an expert dancer. One Friday night he drove with her down to Squaw Bay and parked.

During a heavy "petting" session, Ruth suddenly drew back, looked directly at him, and exclaimed, "You can have me or you can have Noel. You can't have both!"

Jesus! How the hell did she know about *that!* "To hell with you! he yelled and in total silence drove her home. He never dated her again.

Once or twice a week Buddy and Noel went by themselves to Squaw Bay, taking large bath towels to stretch out on after their swim. Buddy would dry Noel's hair with one towel and then would tousle it with his right hand. That summer Noel had read the life of Oscar Wilde, had reread *The Picture of Dorian Gray,* and knew that what he felt had been felt before and had been done before. He was not alone. If only he had a picture to put up in the attic.

Miriam and three other girls were learning to play bridge. They played bridge twice each week; they went to the Capitol Theater on Saturday afternoon. And they occasionally accompanied the Saturday night crowd to the Cricket. To them it did not have the glamour of their safe Legion Hut dances, and unrestricted crowds there intimidated them. The American Legion raised money and built a tennis court in the south part of town. Not many of the teenagers came to play tennis because a tennis racket and tennis balls proved too costly.

September came and life changed for many in Melville. Abe Stein was clearing a space in his office for his cotton-buying activities. He was exhorting Fatty Maxton to get those Negroes up early and into the fields for the harvest. This had been a good crop year, and Abe was anxious to start gathering the profits.

Buddy McAimes and Noel left for Teacher's College in Conway. Miriam left for St. Louis and Washington University. The young of the human race were moving relentlessly forward toward tomorrow. One of the 1935 graduates managed to go to the University of Arkansas. It seemed, and it was, a world away from Melville.

18

Miriam graduated from Washington University in St. Louis and returned home to announce that she planned to marry Karl Lewis, a Jewish boy from New York, whom she had dated at the university. Her mother, Sarah, immediately started planning a garden wedding for December—in a small flower garden she maintained on the east side of her home. On December 20th, the wedding ceremony was performed by a rabbi brought from Helmsman, the county seat, twenty miles east of Melville.

Everybody in Melville who was anybody was invited. Mary Pollard Bracken came bringing her seven-year-old son, Pollard. Billy Bracken did not attend. Dave Pollard and Josephine came. Just one month before, Mrs. Dave Pollard, Sr. had died and Dave and Josephine had been married in Helmsman by a justice of the peace. Joe Wener and his wife were there. Carrie, the Stein's maid, was there in a new maid's uniform, and Sarah had also hired Earnestine, Billy Bracken's former housekeeper, to help with the crowd.

When Billy Bracken married Mary, Earnestine had moved back in with her mother. Two months before Billy's son, Pollard, was born, Earnestine gave birth to a light-skinned boy. She had named him William and she stared down anybody who asked her why that name.

The reception was held in the Stein home. The crowd was large, but Sarah had arranged for them to enter by the front door, through the living room to the dining room, and then exit through the den and out the side door. Abe Stein was everywhere, smiling, shaking hands, and slapping backs.

The record player, with an automatic record changer, was turned on low in the living room. Records by Harry James, Gene Krupa, and Glen Miller filled the house alternately with romantic ballads, soft swing, and jitterbug music. It was a big, happy occasion.

Miriam and Karl drove to Memphis and boarded a flight to New York City for the honeymoon. Abe had "fixed up" an older home next door to his for them to occupy when they returned.

Behind Abe's store were four other buildings, including the post office, all of which belonged to Abe. One of the tenants in a smaller store had just moved. Abe decided to stock that store with furniture and linoleum and to turn it over to Karl when he returned from the honeymoon. That way Karl could earn a living, and Abe would have his daughter, Miriam, near him and Sarah.

Abe now owned a part interest in several cotton gins in Melville and out in the country. Each paid him a small dividend, and he had a lock on buying the cottonseed for Swift & Company. There was one fly in Abe's ointment. A man named Roy Skinner had started a co-op gin and was trying by any means possible to attract the farmers to his gin. Once he had handbills made up and distributed, that proclaimed in bold type—Gin at the co-op, the gin without a JEW. Abe was furious. He sent Karl, Annie Mae, and Jack right behind the distributors, picking up the handbills as fast as they were distributed. He poked them into the potbellied stove in the store, saying he'd like to put Skinner in there with the leaflets. It also made a very hot fire and saved on his fuel bill.

19

Business conditions started to improve in 1941. Lend-lease helped the United States as well as Britain. The CCC camps absorbed many of the high school graduates who could not go to college. Franklin Delano Roosevelt sat in the White House devising various plans to improve the economy and each plan wound up being referred to by its initials—NRA, CCC, etc. FDR, among other things, was called the initial president.

Abe Stein was well on his way to building up the Stein holdings. He bought the two-story building next door to his store for $10,000 and refashioned it into Stein's Department Store. To get more of the local white trade, he stocked name brands—Hart Schaffner & Marx suits, Stetson hats in the men's department, and name-brand hose and dresses in the women's department. Profits from the store and the farms increased, and Abe decided to hire a full-time book-keeper.

December 7, 1941, and every radio in Melville was tuned to the news broadcasts. Pearl Harbor, Bataan, Corregidor all became familiar words of horror.

The local Legionaires, who had followed Hitler's progress more closely than others, remarked that we had to be bombed into joining the fight for democracy. The local young men, already registered for Selective Service, began to be drafted. The Saturday night farewell parties at the Cricket became larger, noisier, and drunker.

Buddy McAimes, who had gone to work in Memphis, was drafted and came back to Melville to spend a week before he left for Camp Robinson in Little Rock, Arkansas. Noel Arm Jr., who had found a job with Montgomery Ward in Chicago, also came back to Melville to spend a week. On the Saturday night before they both left for induction centers, Buddy and Noel went stag to the Cricket, danced with all the girls, and stayed overnight at the new motel in Helmsman. As Buddy remarked, it beat the hell out of the back seat of the car out in the cemetery. There was much bourbon talk of when the war was over—when they would get jobs in the same town and an apartment together, but not in Melville. The bourbon made everything seem possible.

Karl, whose furniture store was doing a fair volume, was drafted. Miriam's uncle, the doctor, certified that he had a heart problem, and had him exempted.

One morning, one month later, Karl stepped out of his front door to pick up his newspaper and stepped into a pile of yellow paint. Someone, during the night, had sloshed a gallon of yellow paint across the front porch. Abe again was furious. He called a meeting of all the family and decided to move Karl and Miriam to Memphis. There he could achieve anonymity and success.

Buddy McAimes took to military life like a duck to water. He joined eagerly with those who wanted to be known as "cocksmen." Many of the crude jokes in the barracks and much of the snickering, elbowing, guffawing, were initiated by him.

Buddy applied for OCS and was accepted. In just ninety days, he became an officer and gentleman—by Act of Congress.

Noel Jr., at the induction center, was assigned to the Navy. Because of his superior intelligence (he scored 147 on the test) and his college degree, he attended officer's school and eventually made petty officer. Fortunately, he did most of his communicating via written memos. This he could do superbly.

Buddy and Noel corresponded but, as time passed, infrequently. The mail between Army and Navy moved slowly. Memories faded and blurred. It had just been a sometime thing, Buddy mused. Urgency returned, and restricted as he was, Buddy began to think about a substitute.

In the headquarters office, he noticed a small corporal, who was always militarily correct but somehow seemed hesitant and unsure of himself. Buddy also noticed that the corporal always kept a couple of paperback books on his desk. One evening Buddy remarked, "Corporal, come over to my hut after chow and I'll loan you some of my paperbacks."

The corporal looked surprised but immediately replied, "Why, Lieutenant, thank you, sir. About eight OK?" Buddy nodded his head and winked.

After the evening meal, Buddy showered and stretched out on his bunk with nothing on except his terry-cloth robe. When he heard footsteps approaching, he let the robe folds slide off both sides of the bunk. The one 40-watt bulb gave off very little light, and shining from the foot of the bunk, made a large round shadow that extended above his belly button.

The corporal entered. He took one look and knelt beside the lieutenant who reached over to tousle the corporal's hair, gently guiding the corporal's head onto his naked belly. *Jesus,* thought Buddy, *this one's better than Noel.*

Buddy jumped with surprise and pleasure as the corporal sucked his nuts and then started nuzzling below them. Full mast! Half mast! No mast! One more time!

20

On April 19, 1942, U.S. forces on Bataan surrendered. The Bataan death march infuriated all of America and each one vowed vengeance. On June 4, 1942, in the Battle of Midway, the American ships triumphed. Now there was hope. The Japanese Navy was not invincible. Then on August 7, 1942, U.S. forces landed on Guadalcanal. Heavy losses, fierce fighting, but, by God, we had at last recovered a speck of land from the Japs.

Back in Melville there were the Gold Star Mothers, the Victory Gardens, the ration books for gasoline, and tires were very scarce. War Bonds were pushed and sold quickly. America had pulled together as they had not since World War I.

November 7-8, 1942: U.S. and British forces landed in North Africa. Rommel was to meet his match. The United States of America had entered the war with a tight-jawed hatred of the Japs. Rosie the Riveter was born—factories sprang up in Memphis, Tennessee, Helena, Arkansas, and even in tiny Melville, the local ladies packed survival kits, rolled bandages, and sold War Bonds. Gasoline was rationed and nobody minded. It was for the WAR EFFORT.

By 1942 the depression was almost conquered. From many of the small towns of America, the unemployed streamed toward the large metropolitan areas where the manufacturers were—where the "War Plants" were located. Jobs were waiting for them, paying much higher wages than they had ever earned before.

21

1945 July 27: Japanese Minister Kantaro Suzuki rejects the Potsdam Declaration, saying, "It has no important value." He calls on the Japanese to ignore the ultimatum and continue fighting. Suzuki favors peace but is trying to preserve Emperor Hirohito's throne.

Superfortresses drop leaflets, listing the next eleven Japanese cities that will be destroyed, four in the next three days. Chiang Kai-shek's forces in South China recaptured a B-29 base at Tanchuk and began battling for another at Kueilin. The Chinese have retaken eight former Superfortress air bases in two months.

Melville heard this news on their radios and absorbed it more by reading every word printed in the *Commercial Appeal.* Abe Stein called a meeting of all Melville citizens to be held in the local American Legion Hut to promote the sale of War Bonds. He started the meeting off by purchasing a $1,000 war bond for Miriam. The meeting and the sale were a huge success.

22

1946: By January most of the draftees had returned to Mel-ville—some returning to former jobs, some taking time out to assess their future. Several, taking advantage of the GI Bill, had decided to go to college.

Sam Meter, a local farmer's son, approached Abe Stein, asking for a loan to help him operate a sawmill. Abe quickly recognized the possibility of profits and, even if it was a small amount of money, Abe insisted they incorporate, with Abe as a full partner. After a few years, the business had made good profits, and they changed the name to Meter Lumber Company. Sam was notoriously tight-fisted and many of his friends kept telling him, "You can't take it with you."

The one extravagance Sam allowed himself was to buy a diamond solitaire ring that cost $15,000. He never removed the ring—not even when bathing.

When Sam Meter died of a heart attack, his wife decided to leave the ring on his finger while the casket was open for viewing, and she instructed the undertaker to remove the ring before he closed the casket.

After the funeral she turned to the undertaker and asked for the ring. The undertaker had forgotten to remove it. Sam's friends said, "Well, Sam was trying to take it with him." The next day, with a court order, the undertaker dug up the casket and retrieved the ring for Sam's wife.

In April 1945, Buddy McAimes, while stationed in

Clarksdale, had married a local girl. He was so saturated with bourbon he did not remember much about the proceedings.

In mid-January 1946, he was discharged from service and returned to Melville to stay with his mother while he tried to sort out his life and to plan for the future. He brought two of his war buddies and drinking companions with him. With discharge pay and unemployment checks, they all had bourbon money. On Saturday nights they usually stayed at the Twin City Motel in Helmsman. One was named Charles Polsky, the other was named Frank Smith. Buddy, Charles, and Frank—the unholy trio. Buddy had regaled them with tales of his conquests—including his encounters with Noel Jr., his toy—as he phrased it.

Noel Jr. was discharged in late January 1946, and returned to Melville to stay with his parents while he tried to decide whether to return to Chicago or join Noel Sr. in the insurance business in Melville. Frank had bought a second-hand car, and Buddy occasionally had the use of his mother's car.

Buddy decided he should return to Clarksdale, but before he did, they all decided to have one more night on the town—which meant a night at the Cricket. Buddy knew Noel Jr. had just arrived home, so he called and asked Noel to accompany them.

The Cricket was crowded with returning GIs and their girls and/or wives. The music was loud from the juke box. Many of the same songs were still on the juke-box, except now there were more Glen Miller records and more Benny Goodman.

The dancing was intense, the drinks flowed from the BYOB groups, and many of the girls were anxious to dance with the unholy trio. Buddy and Noel had come in his mother's car, and Frank and Charles came behind in Frank's car.

Around midnight they decided to go to the Twin City Motel. Frank and Charles went into the motel room, followed by Buddy and Noel. Buddy remarked that he was going on to Clarksdale. "If you two want to mess with the toy, you can drive him back to Melville in the morning."

Noel jerked his head around in surprise. Frank said to Charles: "Which end do you want?"

Charles responded: "You know I like the head."

Frank said: "OK, I'll take the other end and we can both do it at the same time." Noel opened his mouth to protest but could only stutter. Buddy left the room and slammed the door. Noel started after him, but Frank grabbed him, twisting his arm around behind his back, and throwing him onto the bed.

The next morning Frank and Charles drove Noel back to Melville. He sat huddled in the back seat and did not utter a word during the short drive. Once home he threw himself across the bed, still fully clothed. Around five o'clock he walked into the kitchen, opened the cabinet doors, and saw a new kind of rat poison containing strychnine. He swallowed a massive dose and sat down in a breakfast room chair. At six o'clock Mede returned from the insurance office and found him writhing in pain on the kitchen floor. She called Dr. Moore who immediately phoned for the Bricknell ambulance to take him to the Methodist Hospital in Memphis.

When Buddy arrived in Clarksdale, he found that his wife (whom he barely knew) was trying to give birth. Complications had set in and the doctor in attendance called the local ambulance to transport her to the Methodist Hospital in Memphis. Buddy accompanied her in the ambulance. She was taken through the Emergency Room, transferred to the Maternity Ward, and put in Intensive Care. Accompanying her as far as he could, Buddy passed Mede in the Intensive Care waiting room, and Mede told him about Noel.

Buddy was apprehensive about sitting around in the waiting room. He went across the street and registered for a room at the Ramada Inn—then he walked down to Belle-vue Street looking for a bar. He wandered into Frank's Bar, ordered a beer, and realized he had walked into a gay bar. Sitting next to him was a blonde boy with bright eyes, about twenty-one years old. Buddy perked up when the blonde let his knee brush against Buddy's.

Buddy: "I've got a bottle over at the Ramada Inn. Wanna come over and have a drink there?"

Blonde: "Sure."

The Methodist Hospital solved the birth complications and Buddy became the father of a seven-pound baby girl.

Noel Jr., in Intensive Care, died a horribly painful death, eased a little by massive doses of morphine.

Buddy, unaware of these two events, was nude, lean-ing back against two huge pillows, tousling the blonde's hair with his left hand. Full mast! Half mast! No mast! One more time!

Four days later Noel Jr. was buried in Melville in the old cemetery where the odyssey began.